SBB

SWASTICK BOOK BOX
MASON OF WINNERS

Cursive
WORD WRITING
Workbook - 2

Awesome Cursive Writing Practice Book for Kids

By: Preeti Garg

Follow the patterns with your pencil.

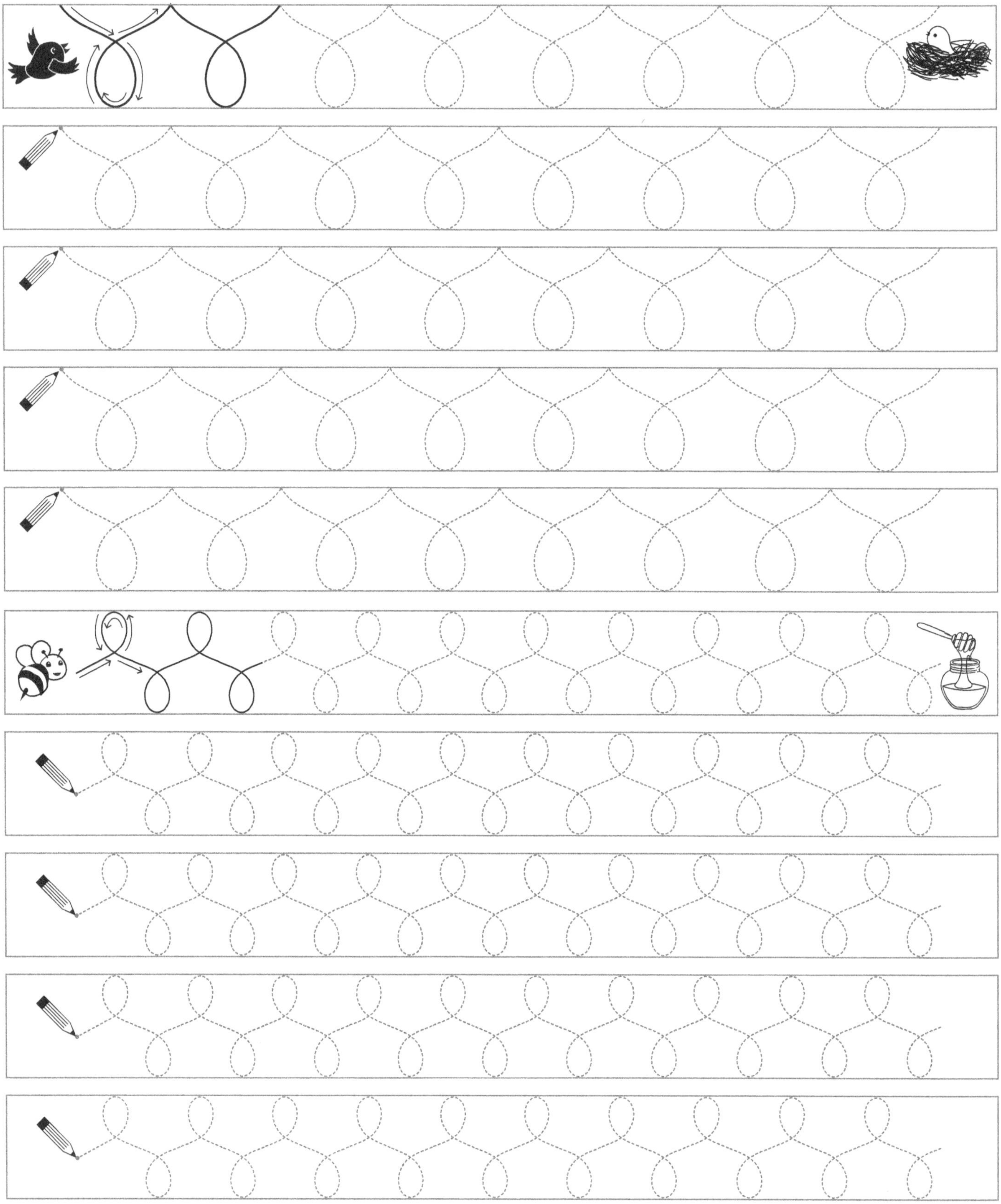

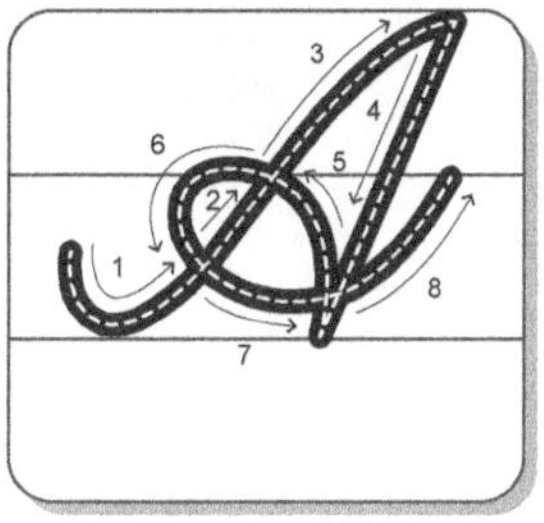

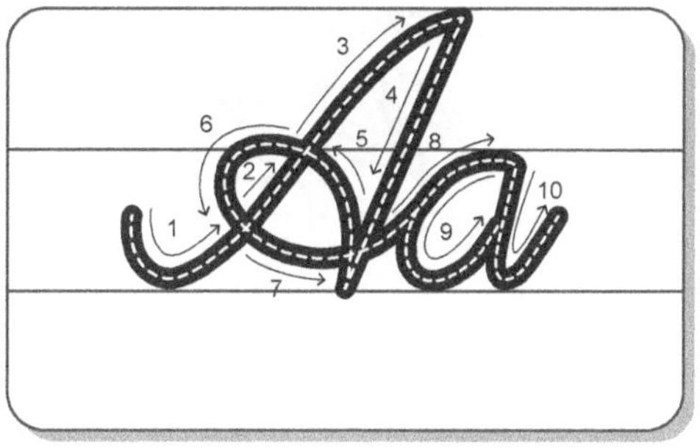

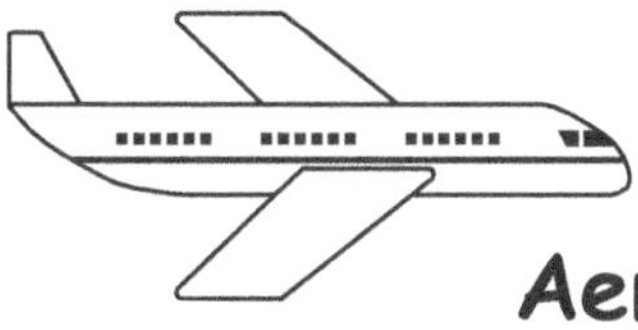

Aeroplane

apple

Date : ....

Teacher's Signature : ....

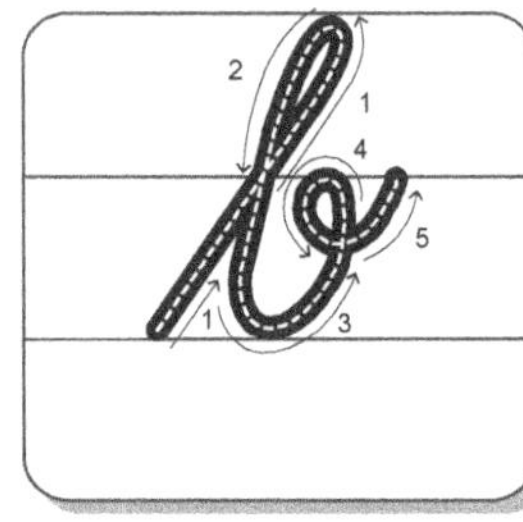

Butterfly

ball

Date : ....

Teacher's Signature : ....

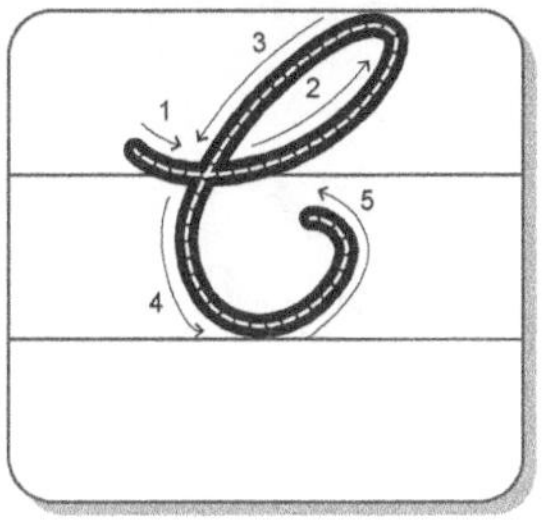

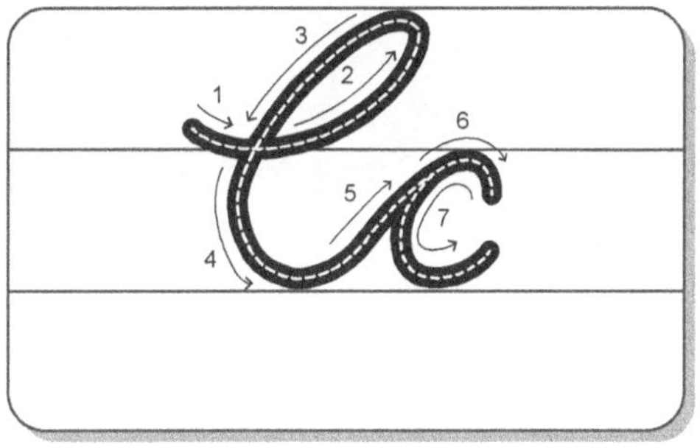

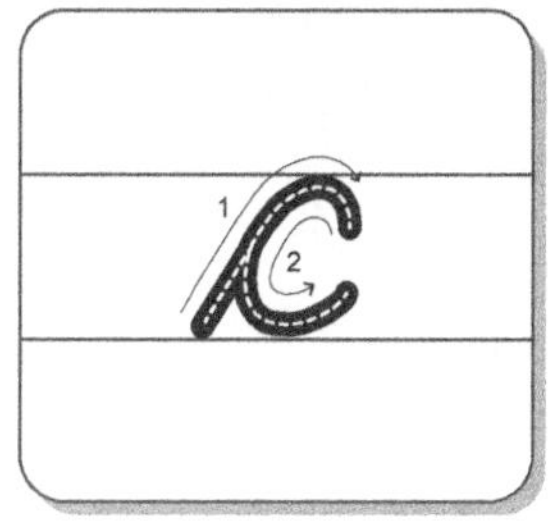

Cap

car

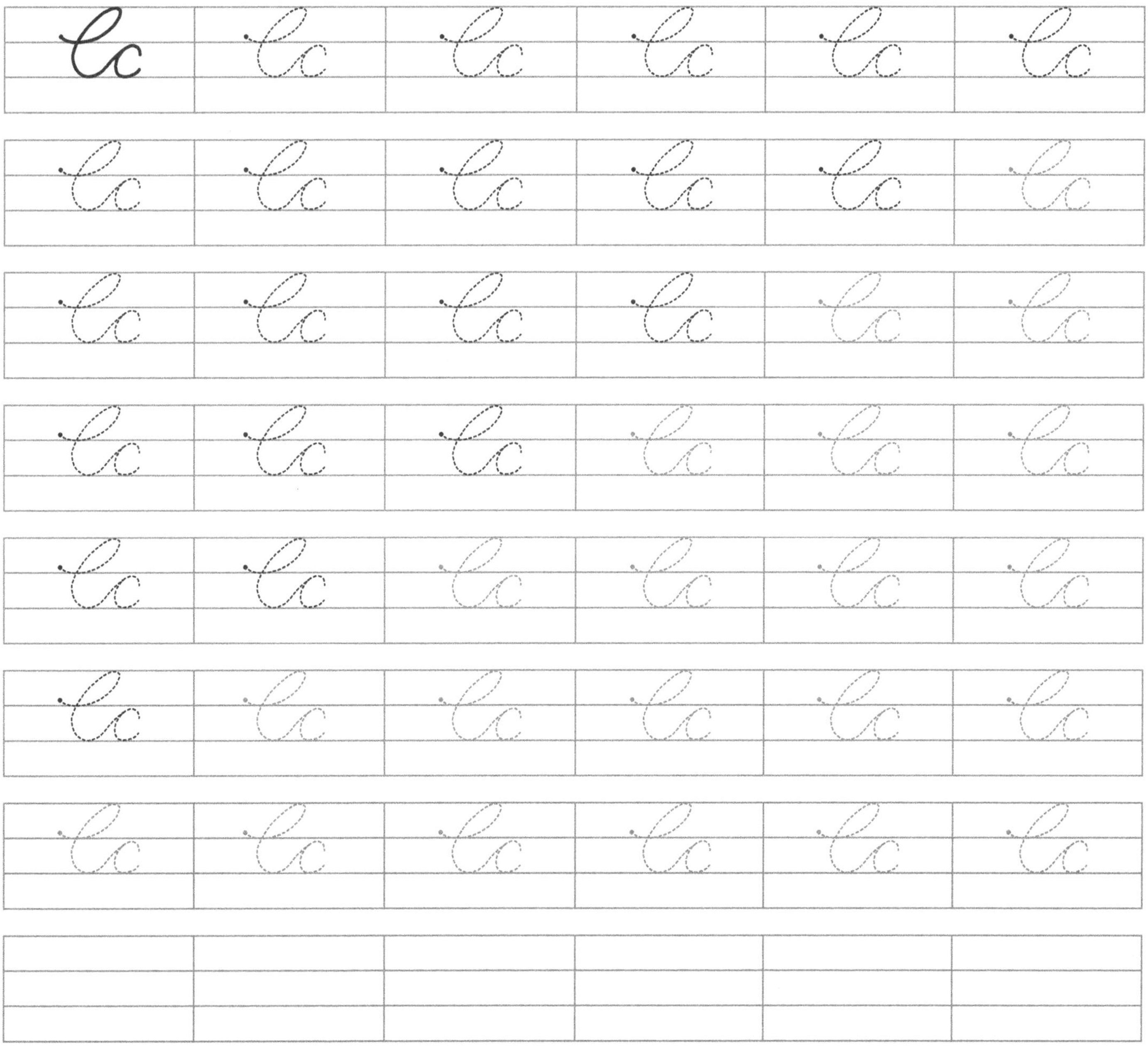

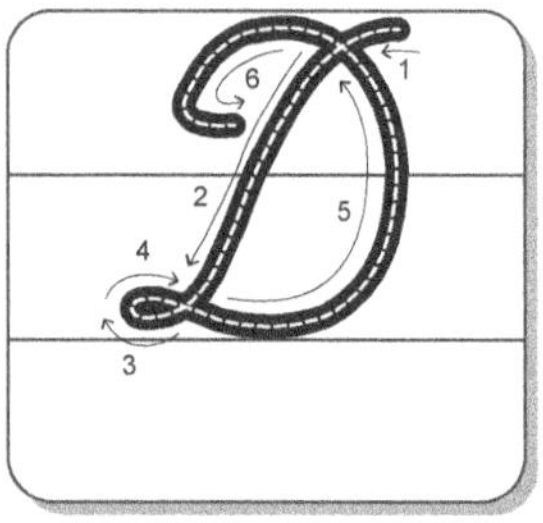

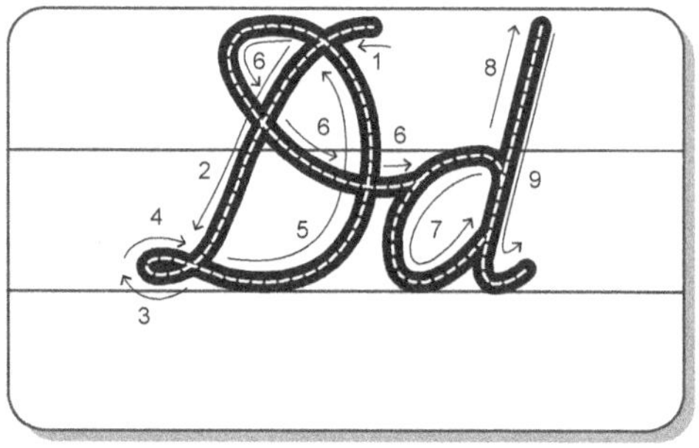

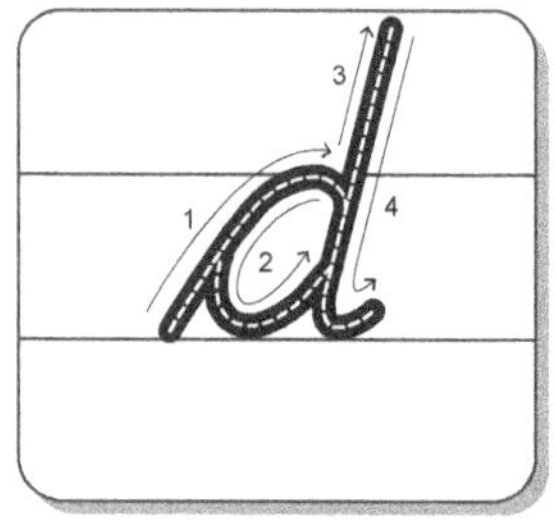

Dog

doll

Date : ....

Teacher's Signature : ....

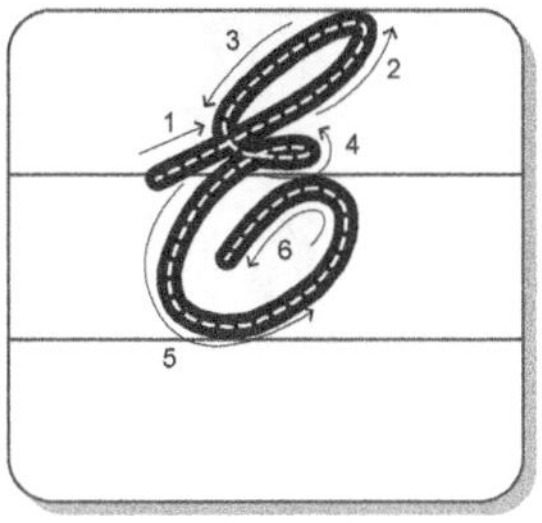

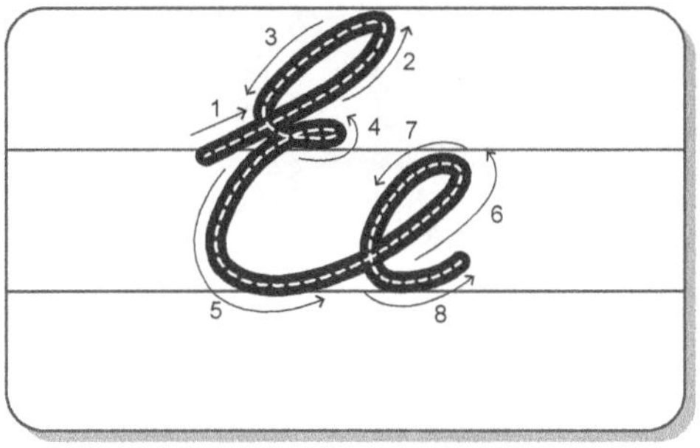

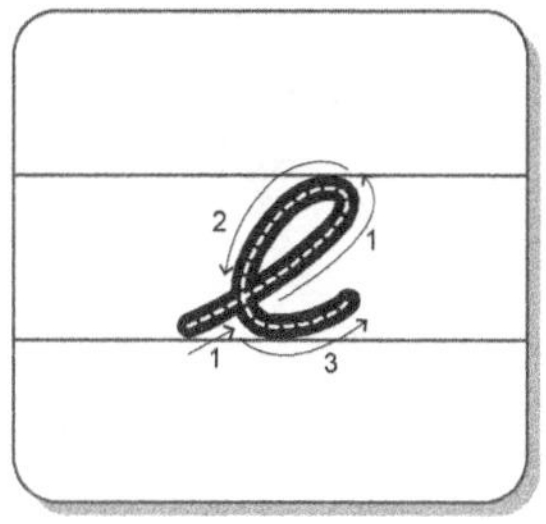

Egg

elephant

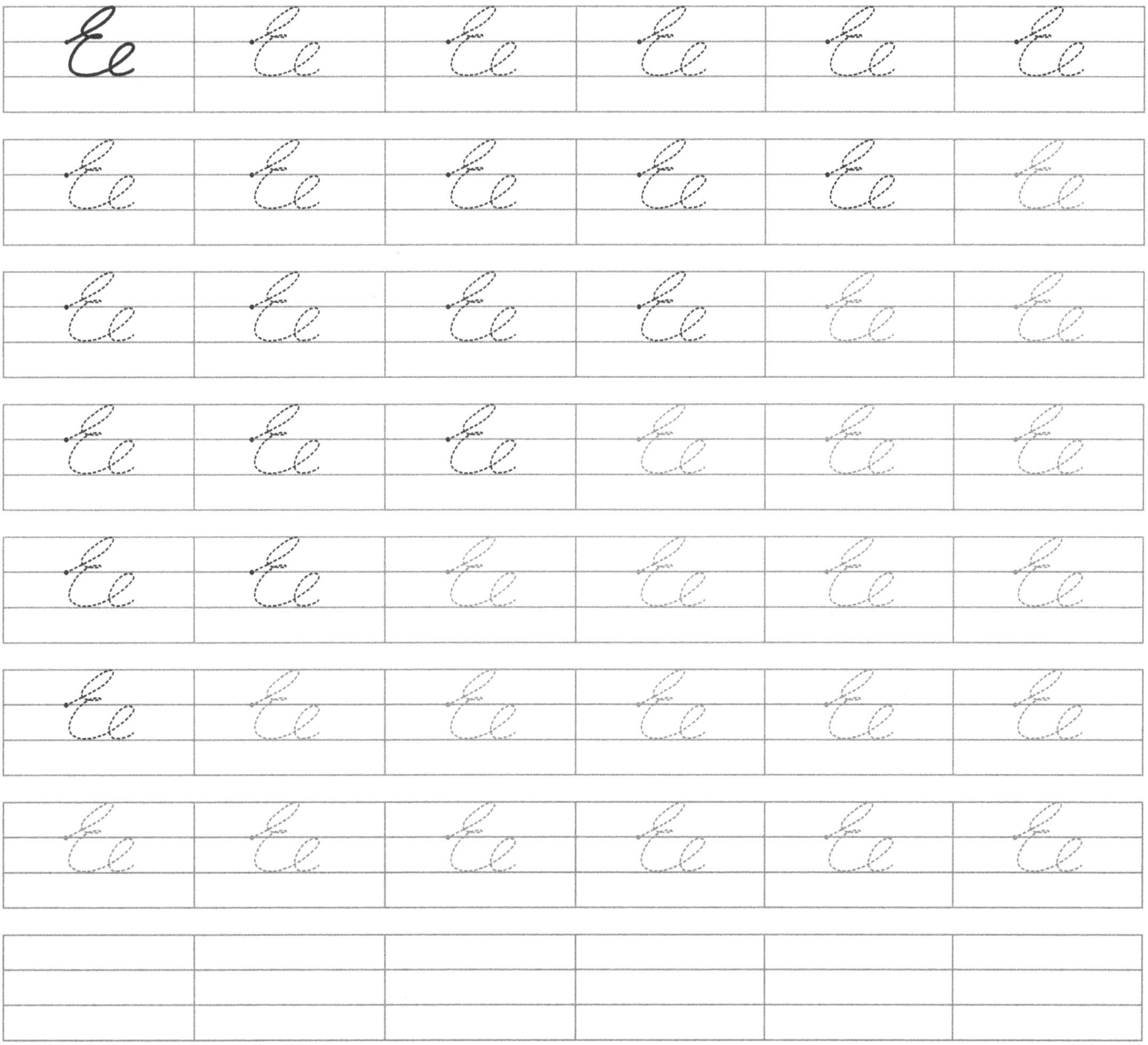

Date : ....

Teacher's Signature : ....

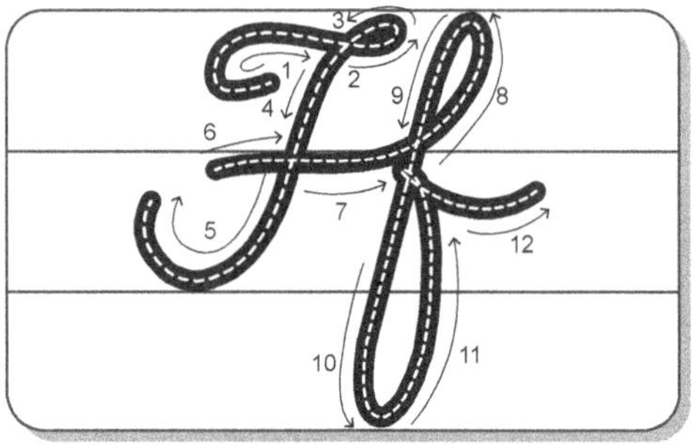

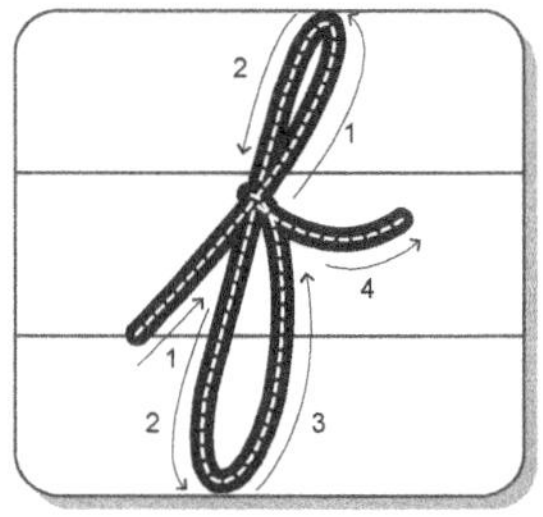

Football

fish

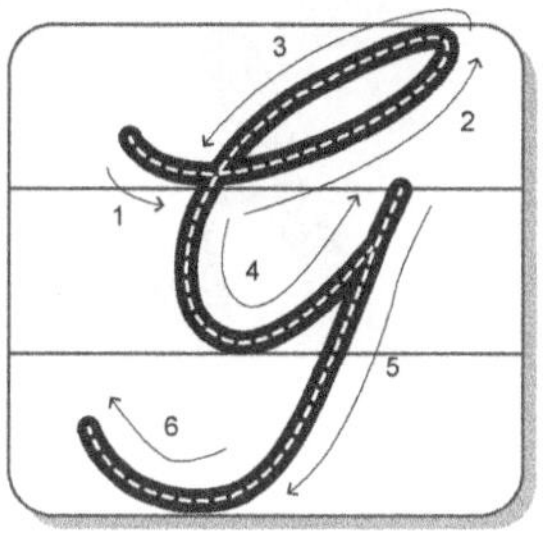

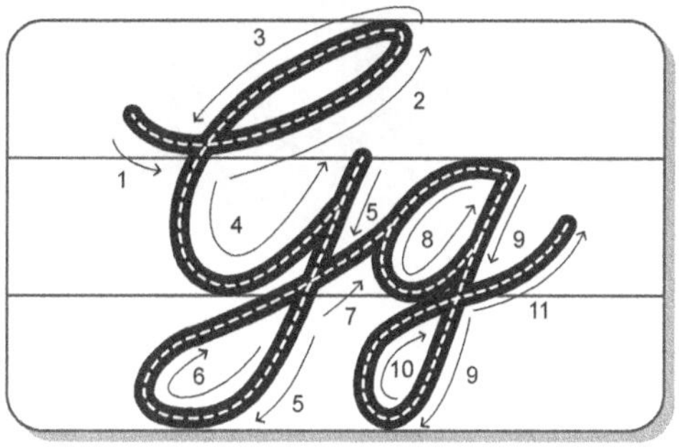

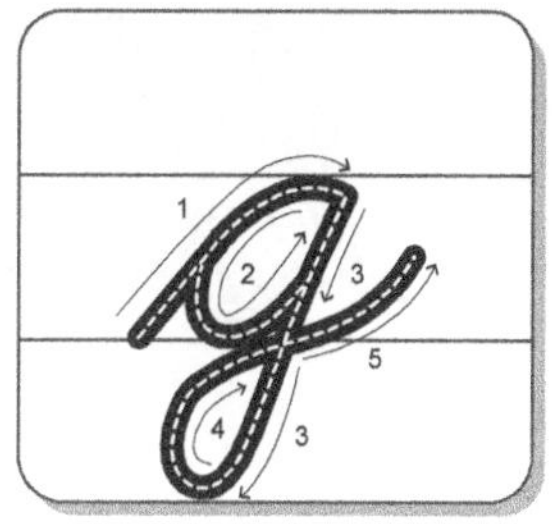

Girl

grapes

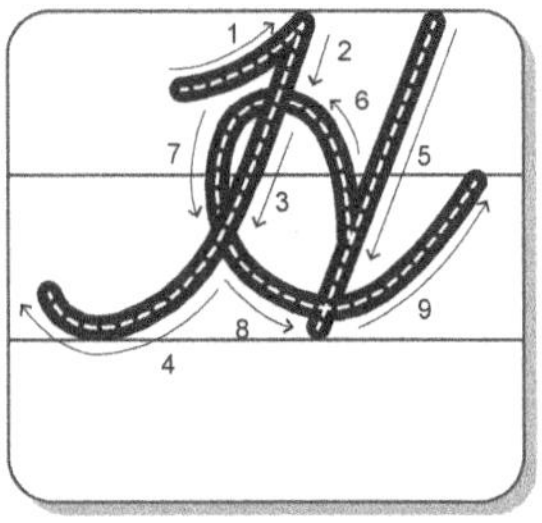

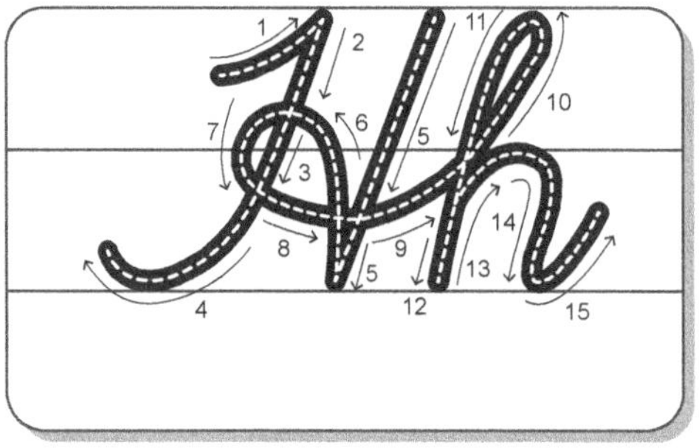

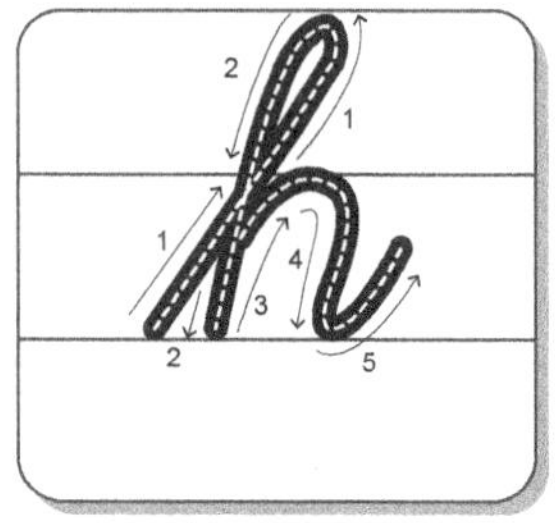

House

helicopter

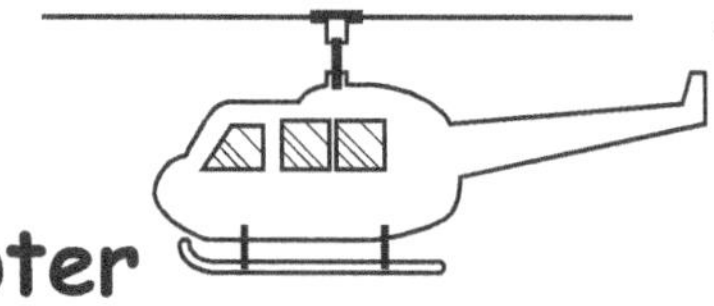

Date : ....

Teacher's Signature : ....

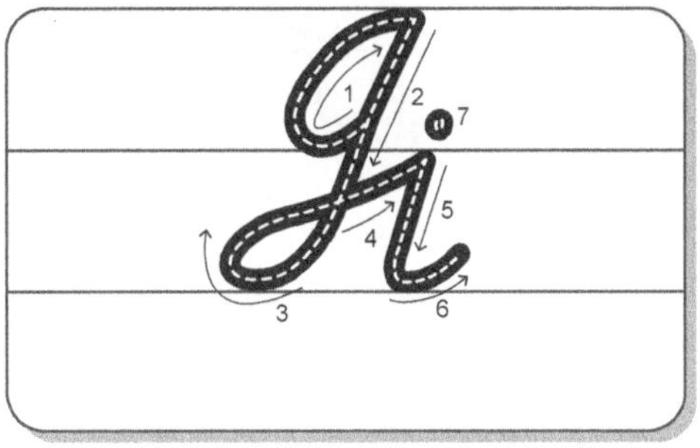

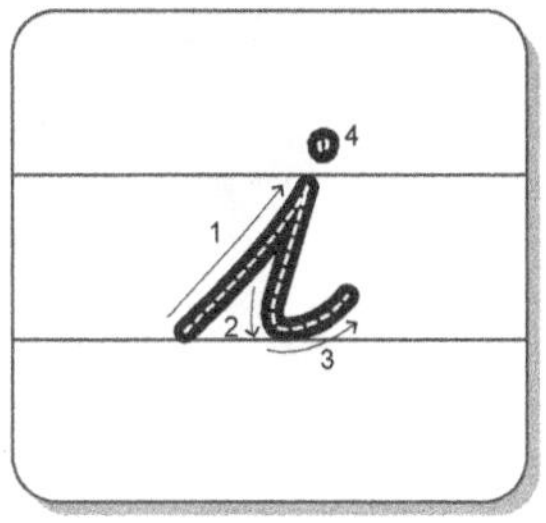

Ice-cream

igloo

Gi	Gi	Gi	Gi	Gi	Gi

Date : .... Teacher's Signature : ....

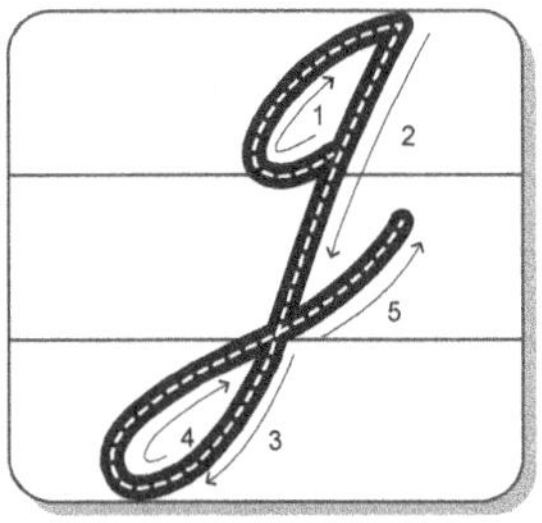

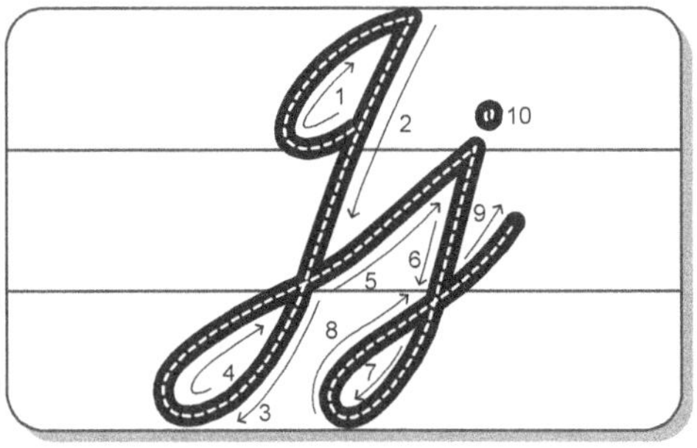

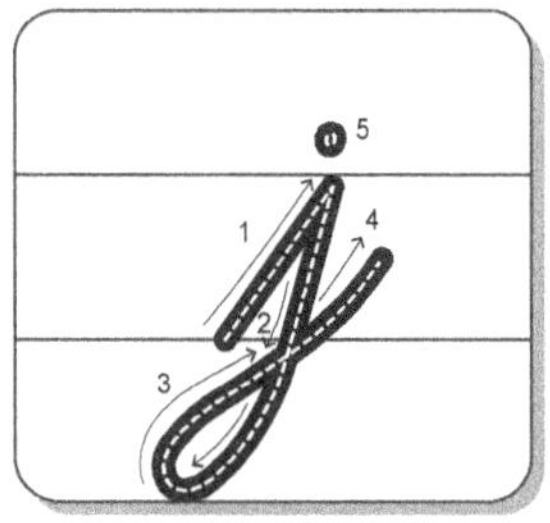

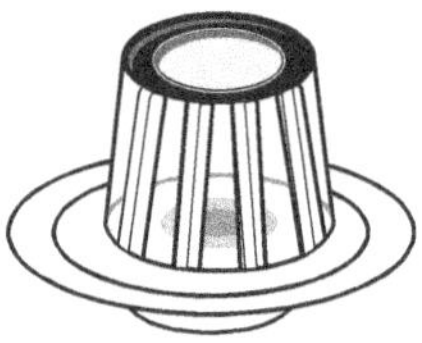

Jelly

Jug

Date : ....

Teacher's Signature : ....

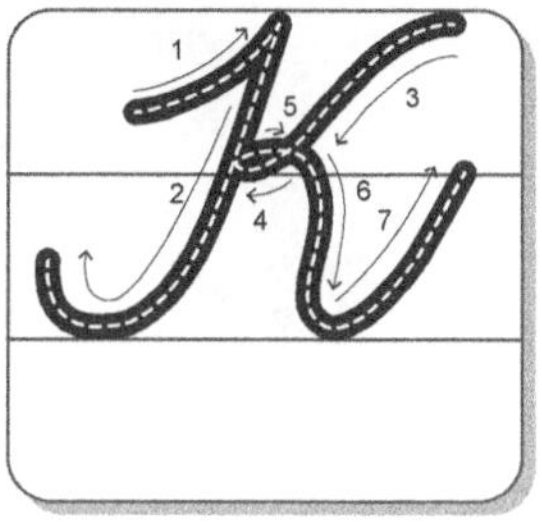

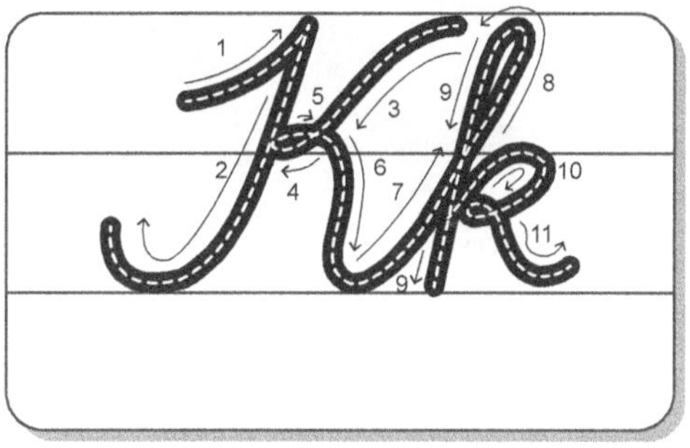

Key

kite

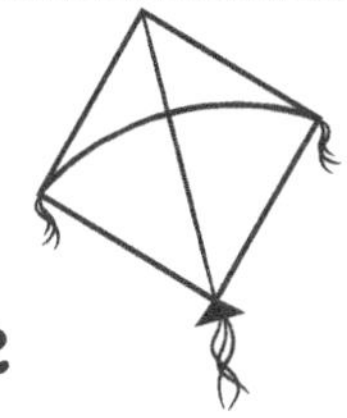

Kk

Date : ....

Teacher's Signature : ....

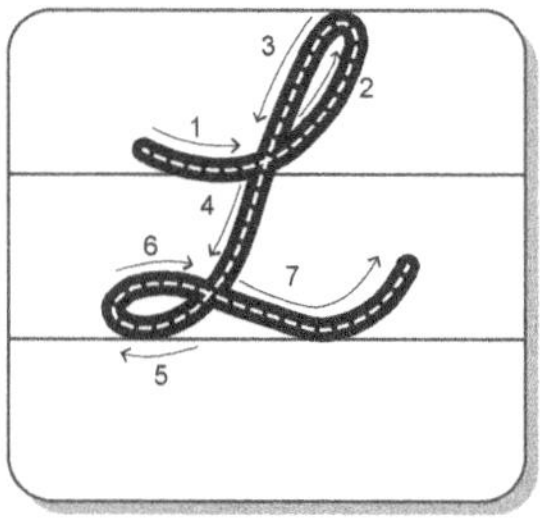

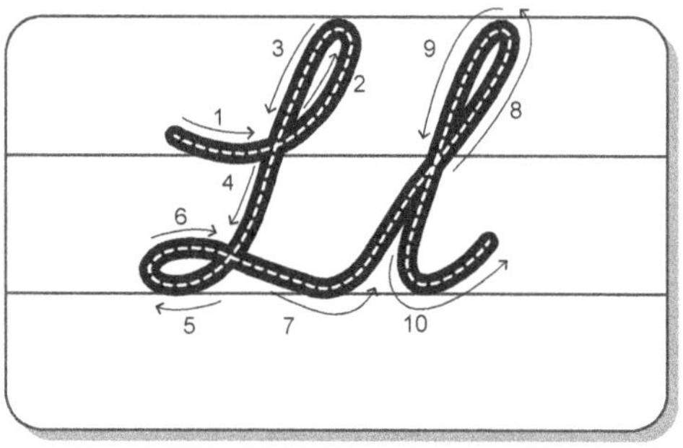

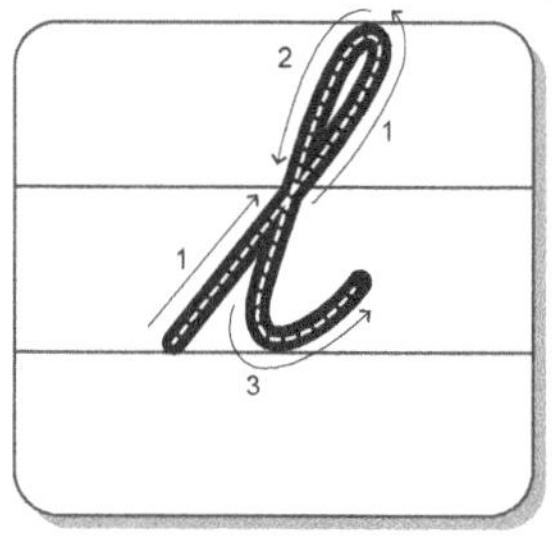

Lion

lock

Date : ....

Teacher's Signature : ....

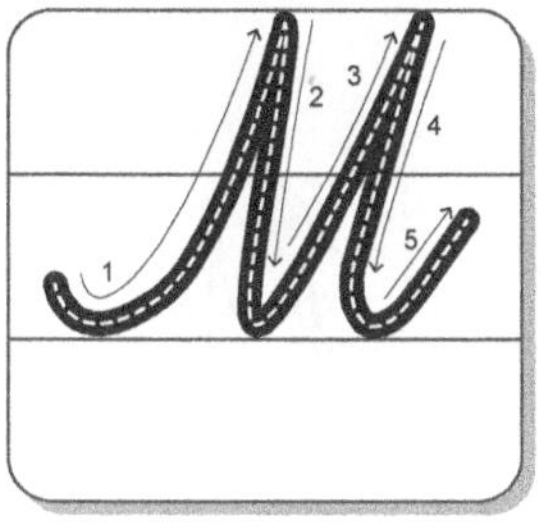

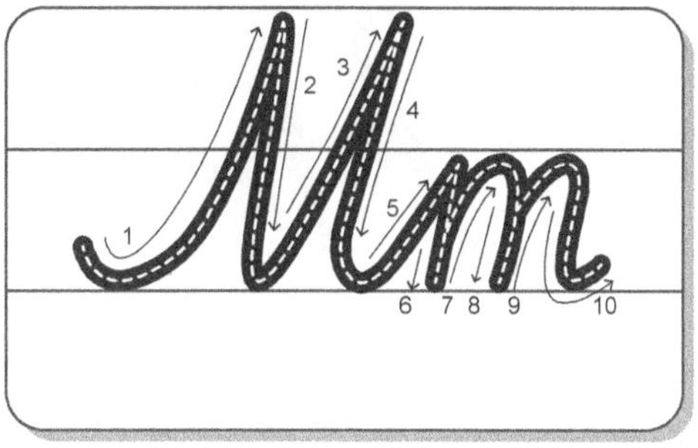

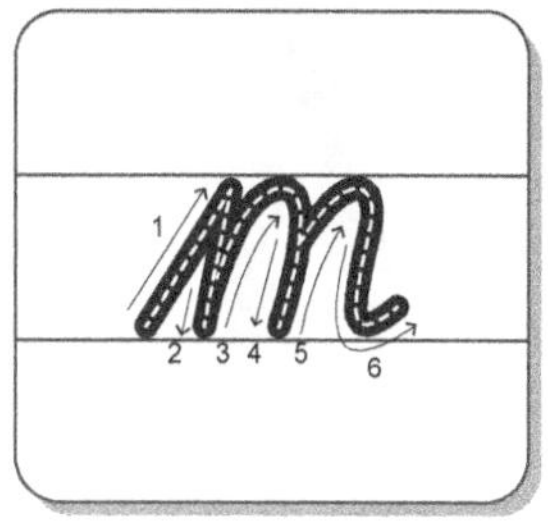

Mango

moon

Date : ....

Teacher's Signature : ....

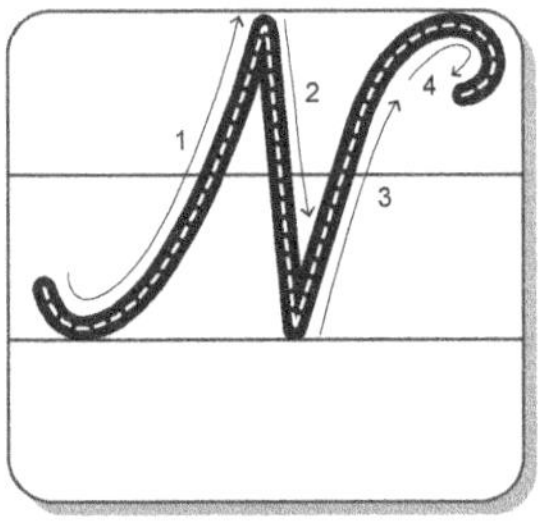

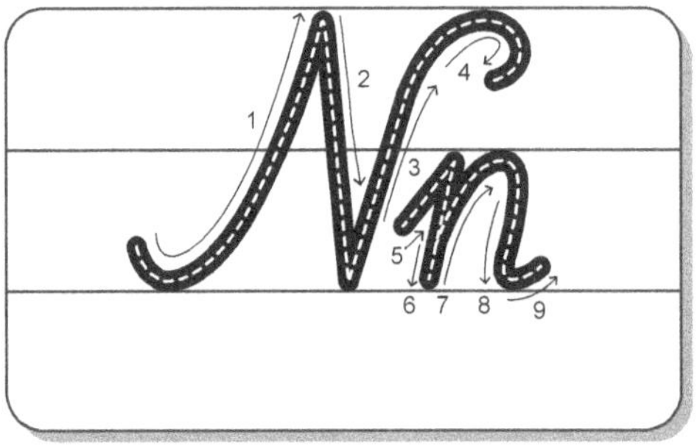

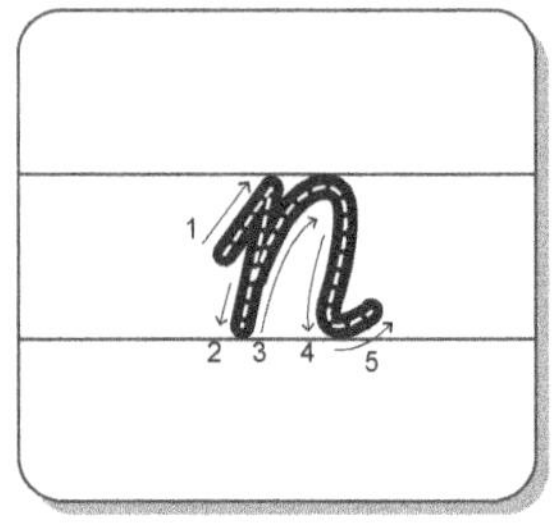

9 **Nine**

nose

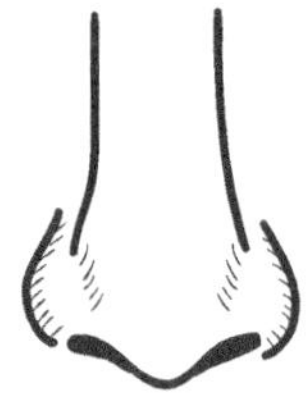

Nn	Nn	Nn	Nn	Nn	Nn
Nn	Nn	Nn	Nn	Nn	Nn
Nn	Nn	Nn	Nn	Nn	Nn
Nn	Nn	Nn	Nn	Nn	Nn
Nn	Nn	Nn	Nn	Nn	Nn
Nn	Nn	Nn	Nn	Nn	Nn
Nn	Nn	Nn	Nn	Nn	Nn

Date : ....

Teacher's Signature : ....

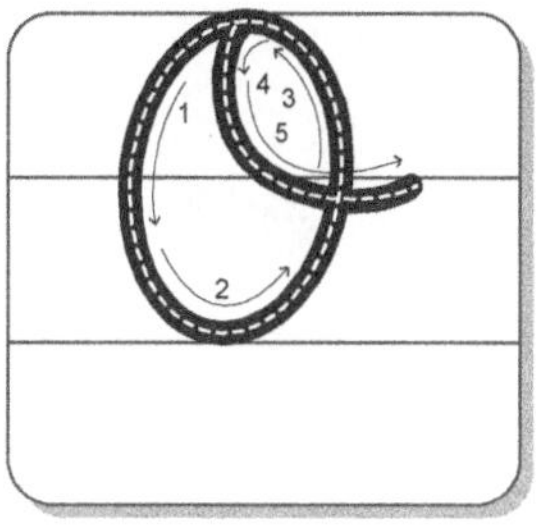

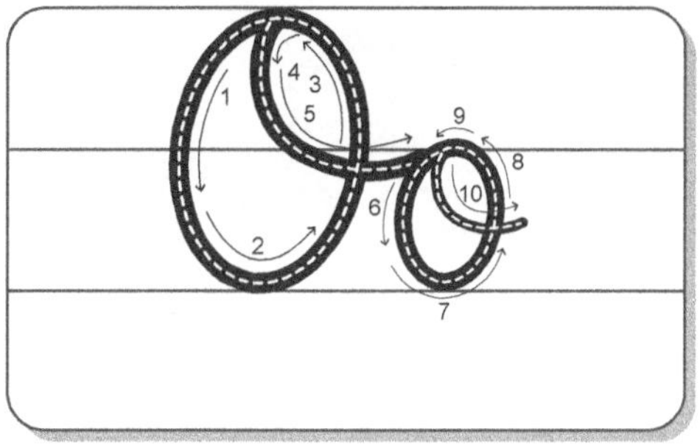

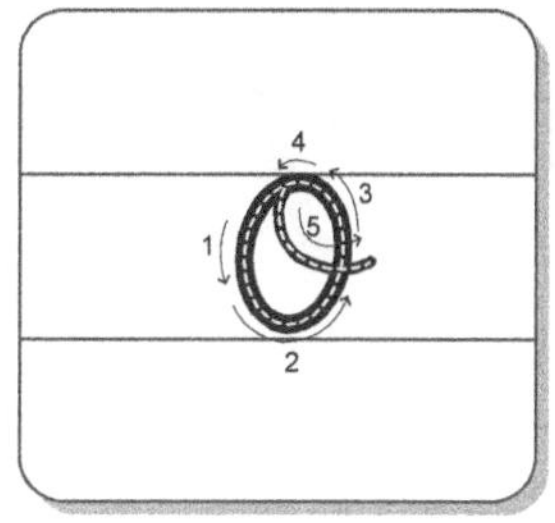

Orange

onion

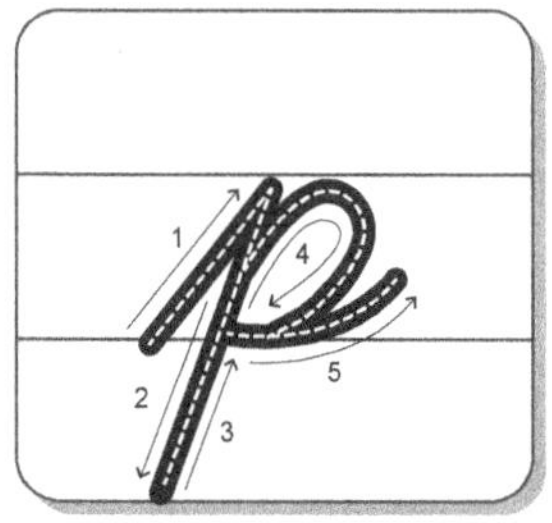

Pool

pencil

Date : ....

Teacher's Signature : ....

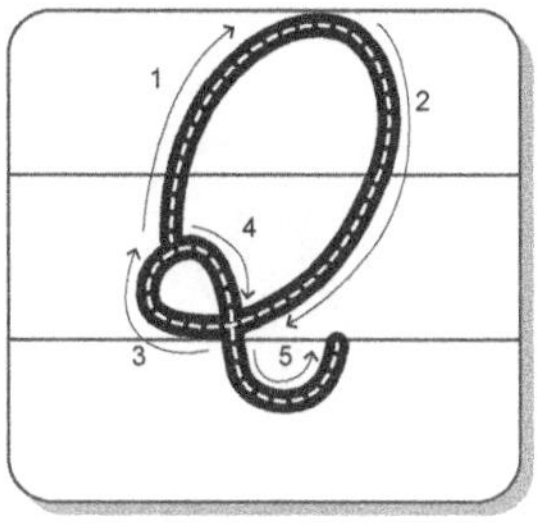

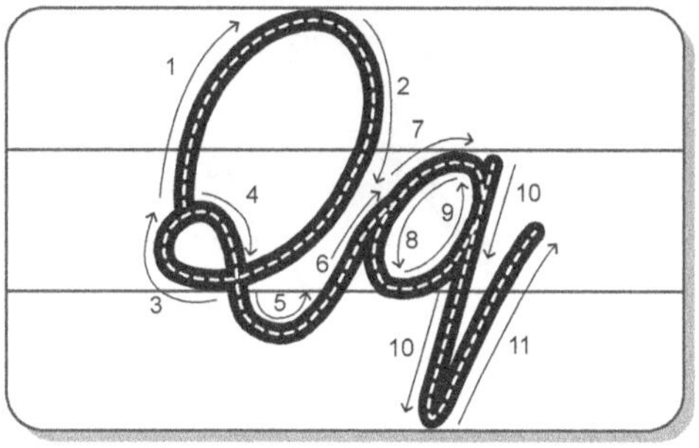

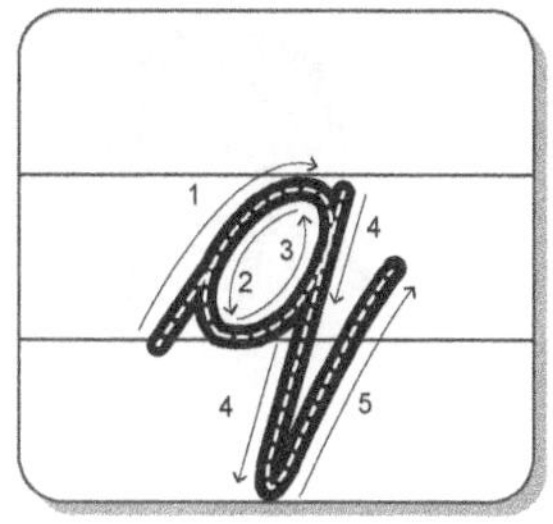

Queen

quill

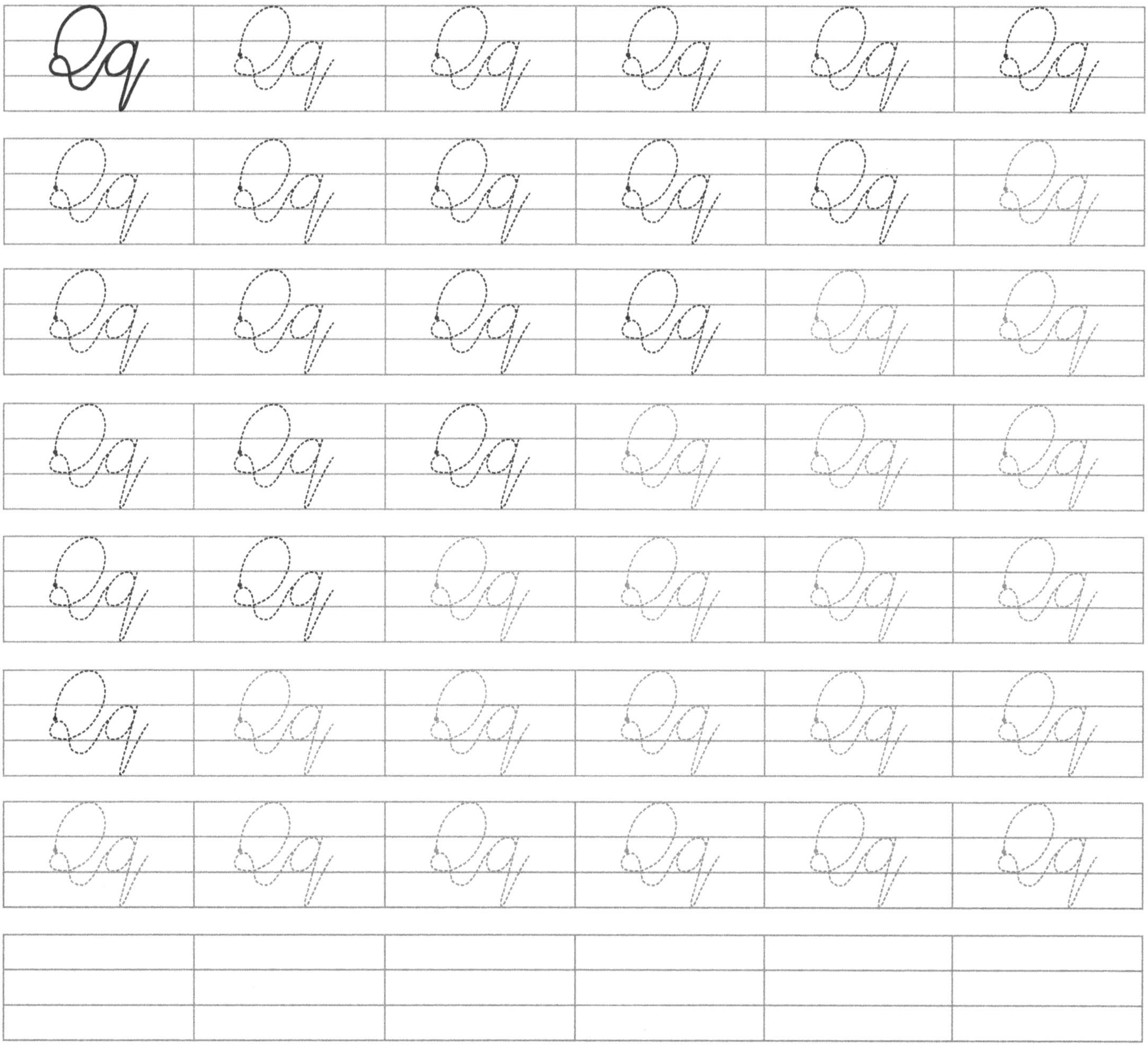

Date : ....

Teacher's Signature : ....

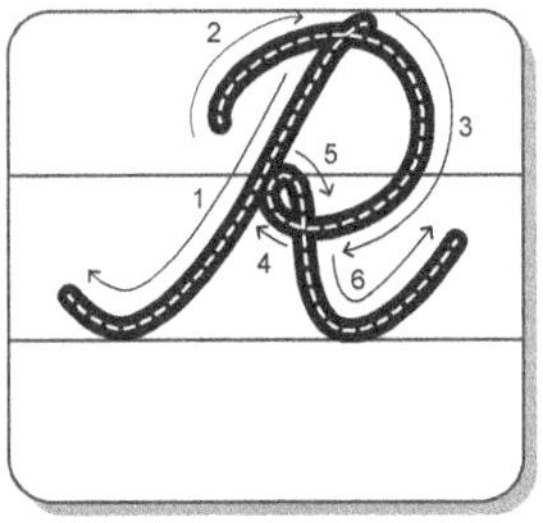

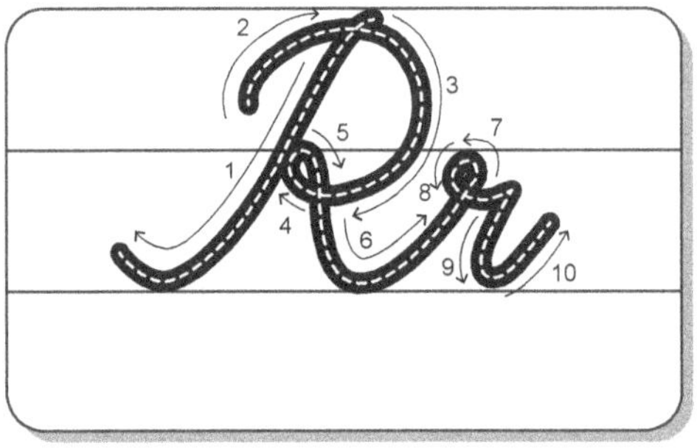

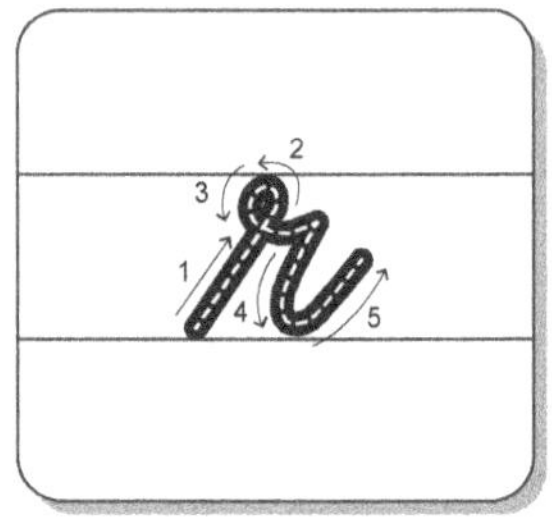

Rabbit

rat

Date : ....

Teacher's Signature : ....

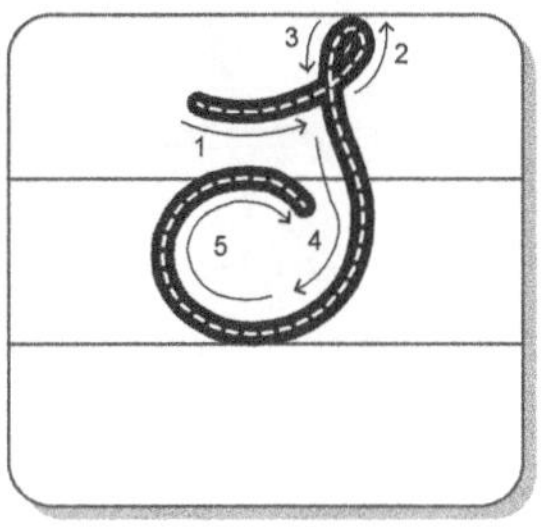

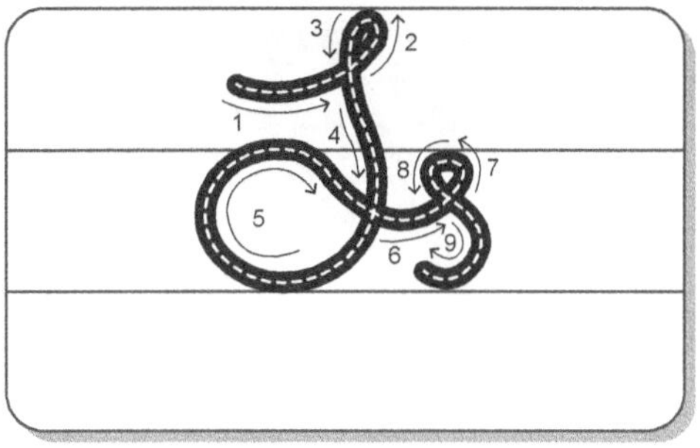

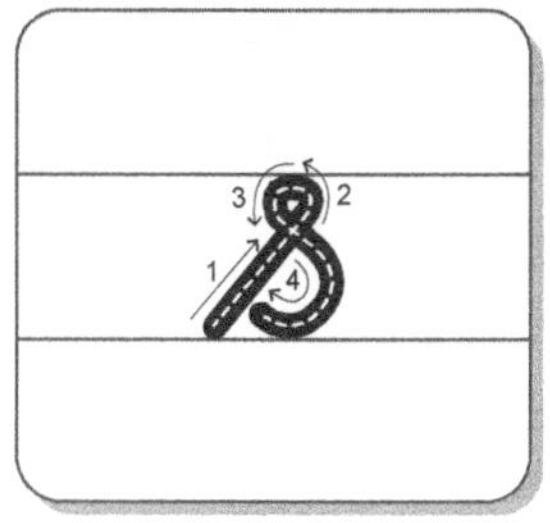

Snowman

ship

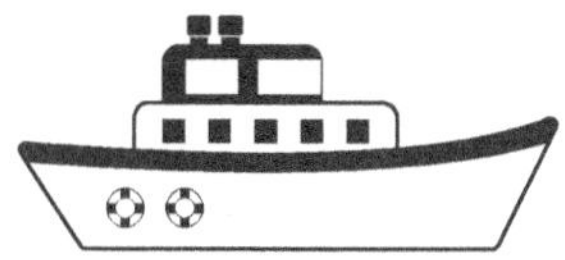

Date : ....

Teacher's Signature : ....

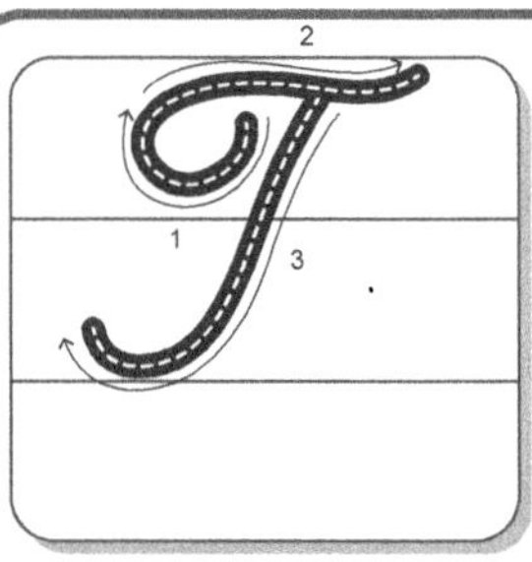

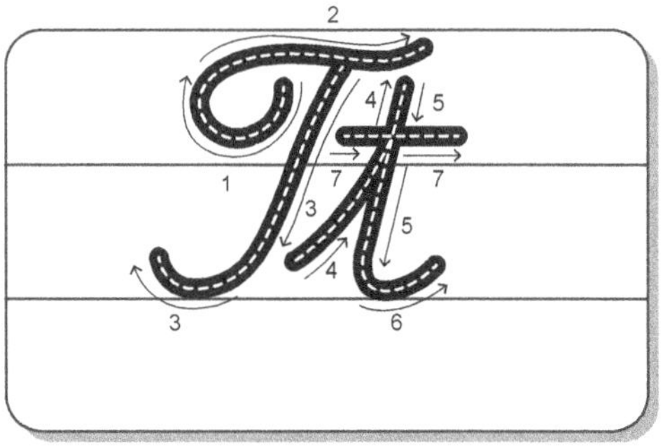

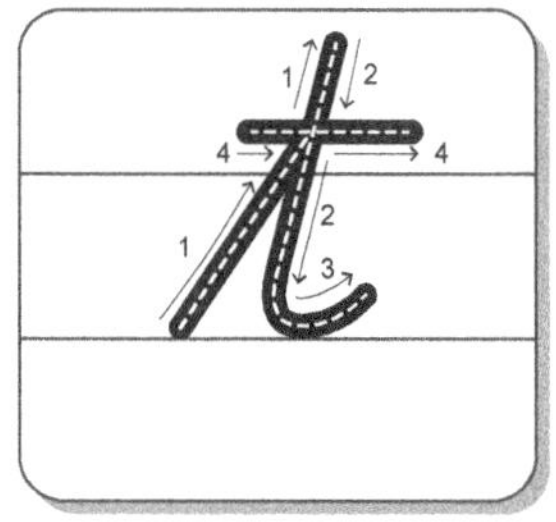

Top

table

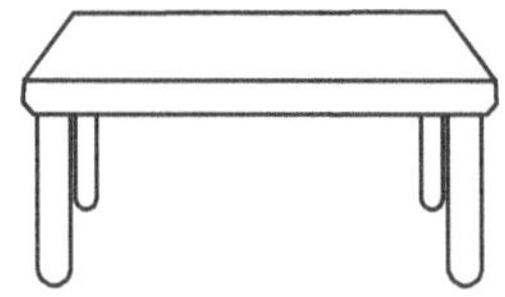

Unicorn

umbrella

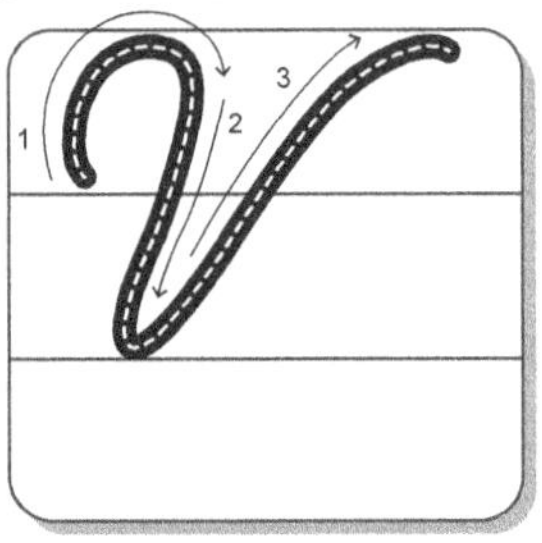

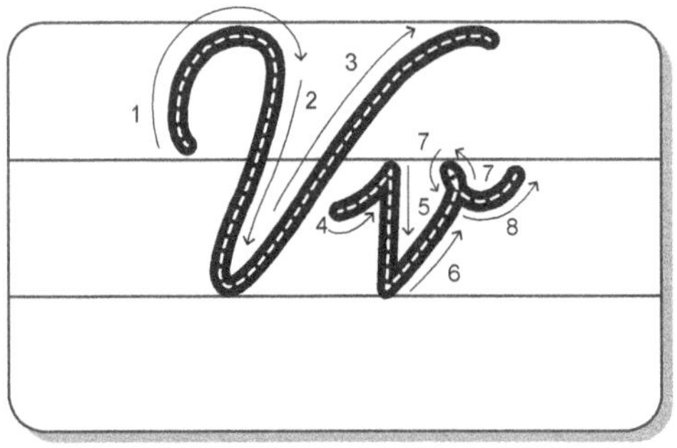

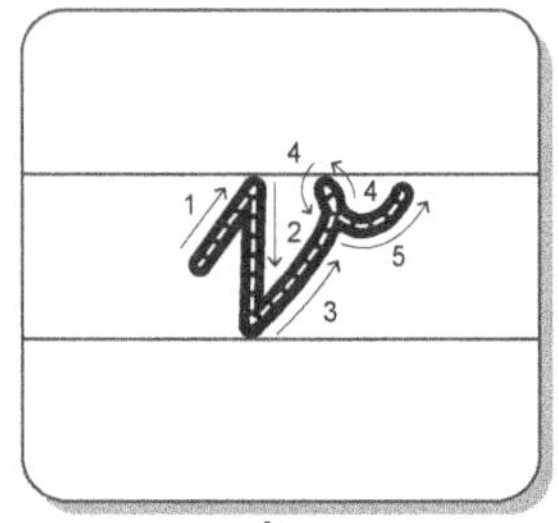

Van

vase

Date : ....

Teacher's Signature : ....

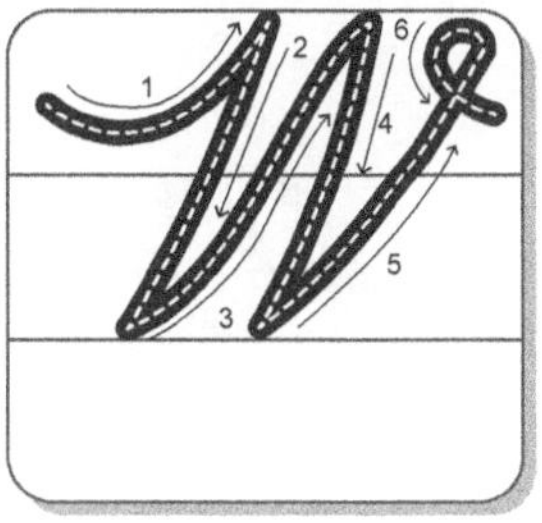

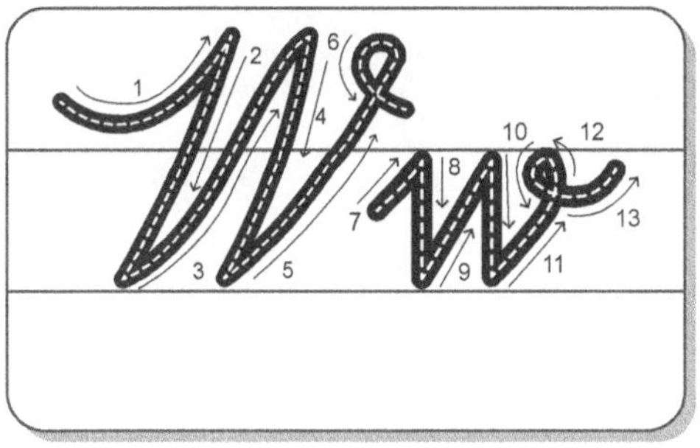

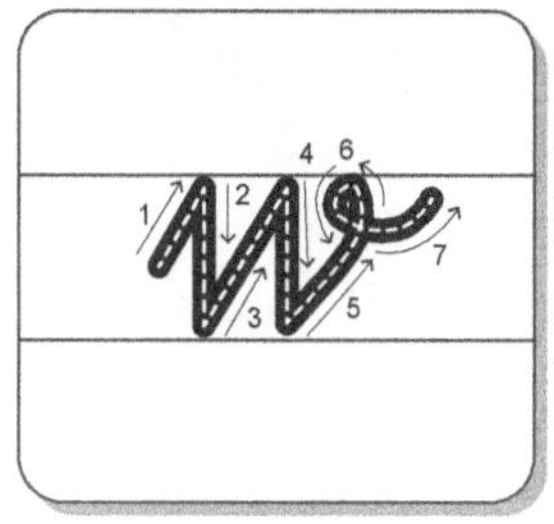

watch

Window

Date : ....

Teacher's Signature : ....

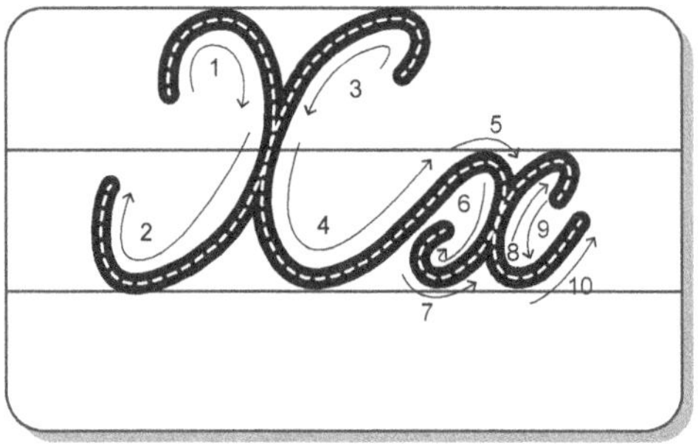

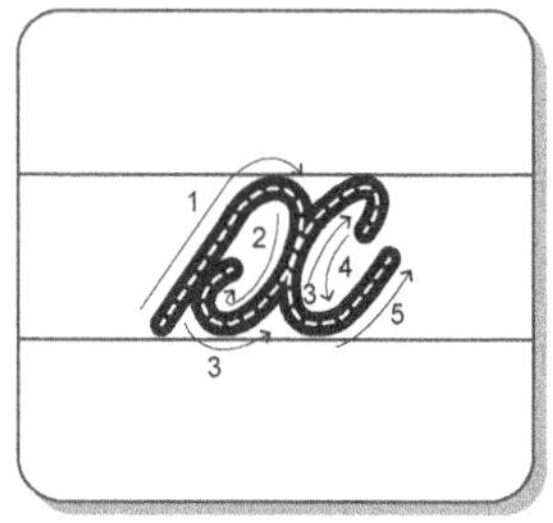

Xylophone

x-mas tree

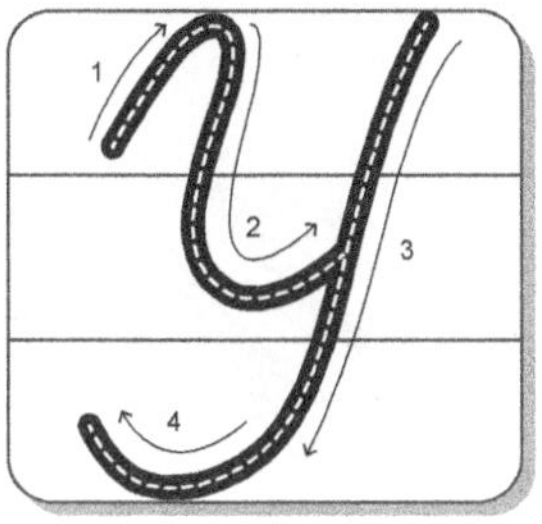

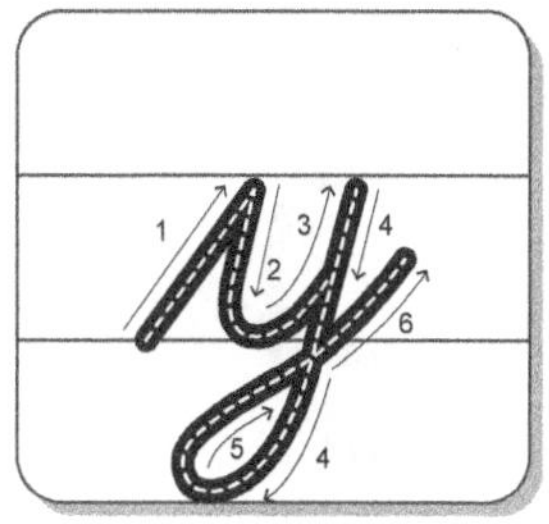

Yak

yacht

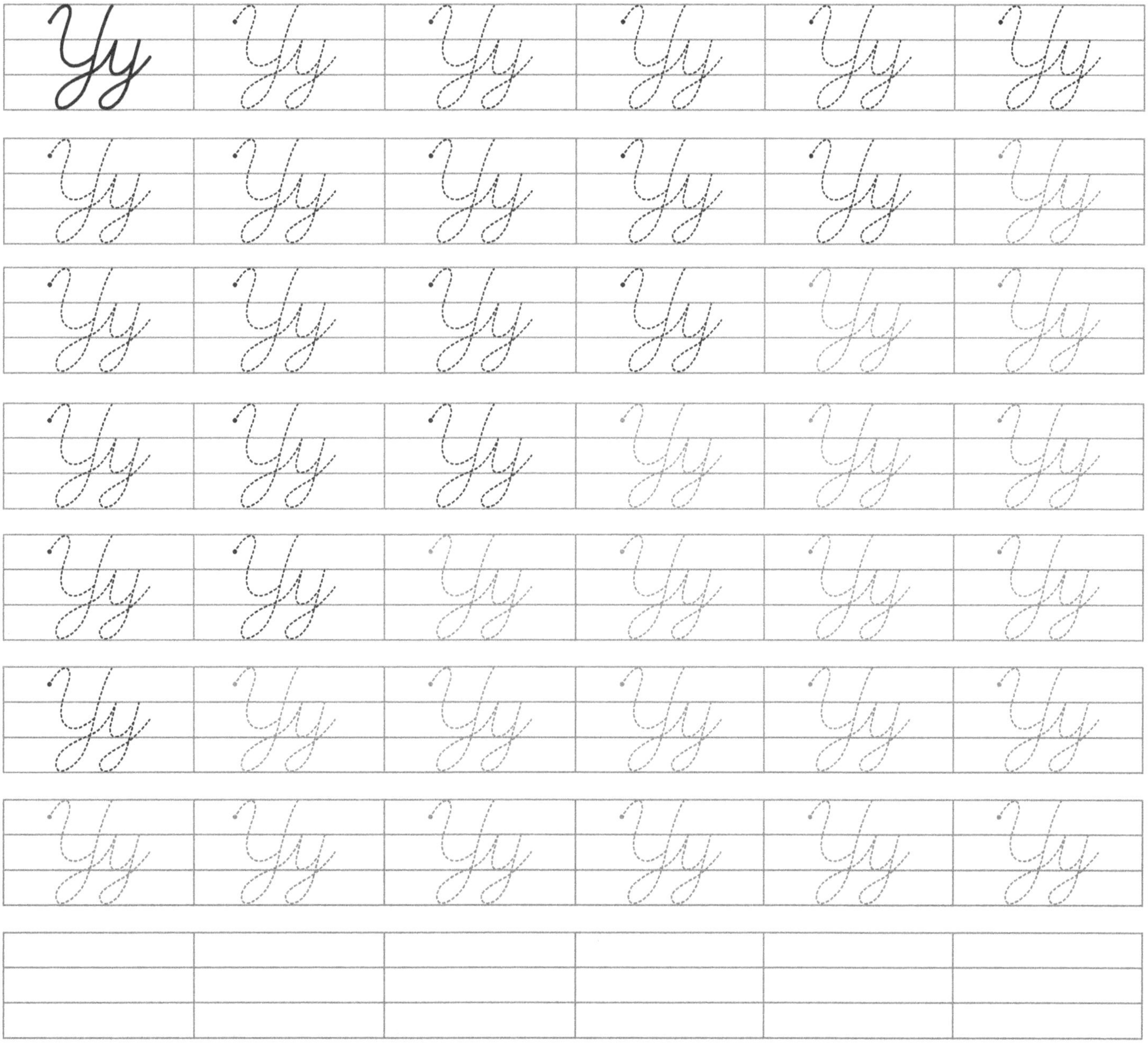

Date : ....

Teacher's Signature : ....

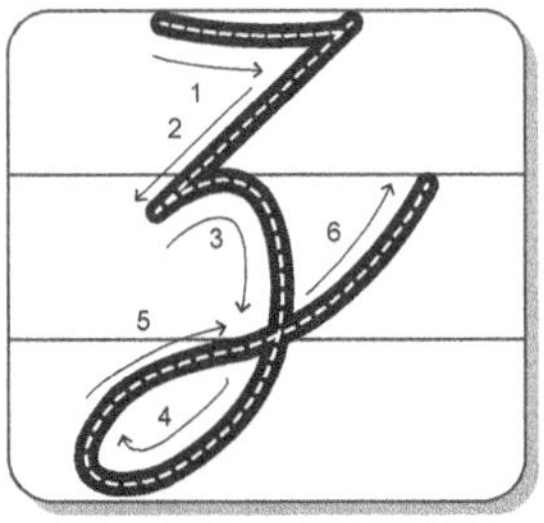

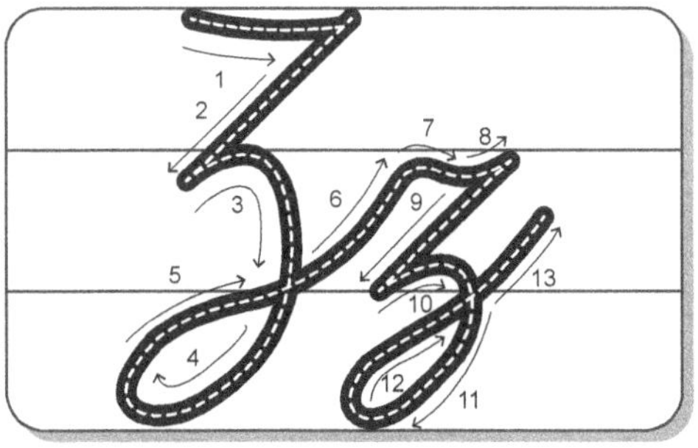

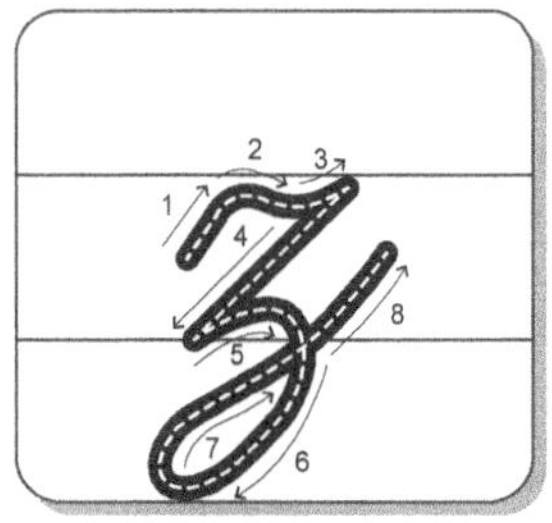

Zeppelin

zebra

Ab Bc Cd De Ef

Ab Bc Cd De Ef

Fg Gh Hi Ij Jk

Fg Gh Hi Ij Jk

Kl Lm Mn No Op

Kl Lm Mn No Op

Pq Qr Rs St Tu

Pq Qr Rs St Tu

Uv Vw Wx Xy Yz

Uv Vw Wx Xy Yz

Am At Do Go He

am at do go he

If	Is	Me	My	No
if	is	me	my	no
On	So	To	Up	We
on	so	to	up	we
In	Ox	Us	Be	As
in	ox	us	be	as

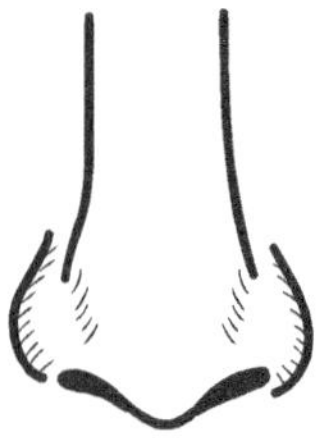

Nose

Apple

N	No	Nos	Nose
Ap	App	Appl	Apple